for my mother, Ayya Gunasari

CONTENTS

"*Nats* are spirits believed to have the power to influence the everyday life of people in their orbit. The vitality of this belief is embedded in the rituals, including people's worship in daily life, the role of mediums, and the holding of *nat* festivals. The list of 37 official *nats* (that were integrated with Buddhism by King Anawrahta in the 12th century) includes only some of them. Because *nats* hold sovereign power in particular geographical locations, small shrines called spirit houses are often placed in a village or even inside or near a worshipper's house where offerings can be made to the local *nat*. As the doorkeepers, guardians and protectors of a home or locale, *nats* are powerful entities. Failure to honor them properly—through offerings and appropriate behavior—can bring illness, injury or disaster on family or community members."

Qiao Dai

A PHD STUDENT IN THE DEPARTMENT OF
SOUTH AND SOUTHEAST ASIAN STUDIES,
UNIVERSITY OF CALIFORNIA, BERKELEY

Spirit House (one)

the *nat*s have stolen my hair

mosquito net winds itself around limbs

watch clumps of black hair blow across the room onto balcony

the house on Inya Lake presses down on my neck & back

smell of jackfruit & sweet orange consoles me

eat semolina cake under crackling palms

hear the cousins gossip: *she is so idle, not as enterprising as her four sisters*

sometimes I cannot bear to watch these sunsets

Storage Unit 202

the rental faces another house
when she arrives there are wild turkeys
in the street
it begins to rain

the storage unit in El Cerrito holds
pinned moths in cases
brass castanets, tin pants
a box of cork buttons

she swims laps in the thunderstorm

Storage Unit 202

1. secondhand gloves
2. a king drinking pear juice trapped in a glass jar
3. wet hair & wet fur   ·
4. velvet spurs
5. directions to the otherworld

Storage Unit 202

I crawl into the pod formerly known as storage unit 202

inside is a quilt made of yesterday's tablecloth, today's plaid coat
· & tomorrow's prayer shawls

the storage unit emits a humming sound

occasionally a high-pitched note bounces off the metallic walls

I cook peas in the pod

I drink moonshine at dawn

observations:

      one might sense a breath over a face

      one may envision the tourists trampling
      the wildflower superbloom

      one can sleep alone with a space heater

Water Space (one)

tree mouth

of river

sculpted ether

incant

branch lip

of sky

mother trapped

in a tree

Water Space (two)

blood hyacinth

evidence of

a past event

childhood

a burning kingdom

slap clap

pearled lantern

bruised hands

clung to rowboat

Water Space (three)

filled the bathtub with warm water

added amber egg dye, marigolds

baptized each other into the drunken night

slept in a swimming pool

rendered in raindrops

sipped lemonade in winter, whiskey in spring

flooded temple, missing guru

child's sandal floating in the backwaters of Kerala

gone towns

Sky Space (one)

the moon appears
reversability

lucent coin
pre-operational stage

stand on platform after stepping from train of eyes
stranger anxiety

dazzling button
imprinting

silent platter
secondary reinforcer

lean against cement pillars
postural control

try to find keys
proximity seeking

car screeches from parking lot
avoidant attachment

stare at sky through silvery
natural domains

skateboarder flips over sidewalk
effectance motivation

begin descent down escalator
reunion behavior

Sky Space (two)

found round stone

in gutter

felt lighter

school bus arrived

stone remained in center of palm

pink sky through window

oval cloud

felt stone in palm & recalled a father

who held a mug

made of gold

wallpaper in dining room a forest to wonder

counted people on sidewalk

girl pulling wagon under freeway overpass

stone cold in hand

girl cold in air

gold forest

Sky Space (three)

a limited edition
annotated records for the researchers

referred to footnotes about the survivors
how they lived how they moved how they breathed

opened door & let sky inside

Vase (one)

sit around the oak table
drink ginger tea

in cracked cups
aster & fuschia

sunlight on steps
blooms in porcelain

hummingbird sight

Vase (two)

flecks of violet flight
waxy crescent moon

reflects glaze
delphinium, star lily

to mark the now
now we pour water

into bone china

Vase (three)

filament & anther
honey ants on corolla

petals loosen, land
on blue linen

dip bread in olive
oil, inhale scent

of wild lavender

Spirit House (two)

my next door prison
neighbor, we can't see
ourselves, garland of posies

slung through iron bars, *nat*
swinging from old rope

can sense us holding our cups
cocks, crosses
teardrop tattoo on cheek

eyelash on pillow, we touch
ourselves, our cells

Which gives the outer pair the heavy look of bronze clothes on statues

mind the maps of nerves
beware statuesque rabbits who have abandoned their stations
use heavy cream to cover the eyes of feral children

oil the statues until they squirm like freshly caught trout
what does it mean to blow smoke through thick walls
use twine to bind two hands reaching through prison bars

When the galley convicts clanked out of the prison in their chains

fainted panted
close up scar scallop
heft of flesh

    goldfleckedspacebetween

two heads
light bulbs
on wire

    matchedaction

roses eyes leather
belt light popped
corks on floor

    smokethroughrain

dirt on bare heels
birdcage flute snapdragon
tattoo dance

    suchdelicatenerves

Desolation appears greater when pinpointed by light

opaque glass soapy
water men under strobe
lights lick smoke

sleep on shore long sea
arm muscles bust out
muse in green gown

hold warm limbs
warp & weft
teeth bleed

pistol in pocket
walled cells
nip at the lobe

The eye may allow some confusion

after Jean Genet

                    dry, brittle, pointed tips of the grasses

convict

      her sentiments now flowed

      interlaced with cobwebs

            resting places

            dandelion seeds

inside a head hewn out of granite

swill it the way men do

            billy goats

gold and purple cave

imaginary jewels

triangle of black long-haired fur

young and marvelous hoodlum

their fingernails crusted with cement

Is that right? You won't forget me?

searing her eyelashes

Cinema

the auteur pops pain pills
hybrid, saga, biopic

adrift in the head room
nat escape, sirens, deep background

close up of beehive in a cemetery
fugue state, reverse shot, tomb fur

montage of lace handcuffs & cardboard boots
choking ocean

Theater in Four Acts

empire of sound
stage abandoned
invisible construct

luma & chroma
spider webbed
lake drop retina

sea birds are fire flowers
sun totems
mise-en-scène

blue light leaks
through flecks of paint
a message or not

Spectre Show

child with a small hammer
the assembled guests

            buttery teeth
            goat mouf served hot

          center of the panel
          young dance star rehearses

steel-encased contestant
clickclick

            rushed to the hospital
            dog bomb & ambrosia

       artificial dreams
       still-beating heart of a queen

Theater in Three Acts

where are the minnows
song of gongs in mini-mall

what happens to the body after soliloquy
mine in mottled fur coat

when does the future arrive
birthmark on forehead in shape of flame

Hippodrome

a bag of lemons

& what she thought was a midnight cry

she longed to sing

think about lemons now

instead think about what

besides the lemons, there were scratching bats

only when she couldn't hear him, he would sing to her

try to remember how he died

nothing to do with skullcap

nor walnuts & golf clubs

she said she was Irish

she said she ate catfish

Reliquary

striped cat's blazing eye
sleeping nerves

towering puppets
distant theater of Barcelona

rock vines
looping gaze

lavender husk
fruit nut

black madonna in glass case
wardrobe of ghosts

jagged edges
pilgrimage

stirred light
roots in dark

yanked from ground
eyelashes like miniature chains

Tomb

first version:
she lies still
the tomb is being filled
with a clear liquid

the liquid has a texture
not unlike gelatin
a poison or preservative
for the body that has not yet expired

second version:
her body rejects the liquid
they keep pouring it in
she keeps throwing it up

an attempt to live
as the hands move towards her
she is drawn deeper
into the tomb

third version:
a triangle of light
appears on stuccoed wall
she asks *what does this mean?*

the figure
informs her that she
is the queen of New York
& her body is to be filled with pith

she puts on the silver
dress & silver shoes
kohl-rimmed eyes

she is on the dance
floor of a nightclub
the orb throws circles
of light on extended arms

Tower

a flying fish
in smoky air
one woman
in cerulean dress
balances on tower
silk scarf over head
a burden to breathe
forest
on fire
fallow deer
wild boar
sloth bear
fleeing flame
tower leans
to east
pivots
moving earth
she coughs
drop of blood
burnt sienna

a tower shakes

Halls

children   not
sleeping   cement
floors   Mylar
sheets   small
bodies   turn
held   sorrows
collected   panopticon

held in cells
how do they
hold

the halls get cold
the children are not sleeping

Storage Unit for the Spirit House

the father at dining room table shades drawn, wobbly throne
the daughters with their brown shaky hands

a forest *nat* haunts the master closet among
the clothes moths, felt wolverines

daughter #1 hiding behind a juniper bush, bright *longyis*
wooden handgun in metal case

daughter #2 sleeps with a long broom next to her bed
mint chocolates under pillow
5am the father drops a cold wet towel on her face

storage unit filled with boxes of LPs, Joni, Dylan, Carly
back cover of *Jimi Hendrix Experience:* on two hits of acid
this will blow your brains out

dusty military jackets, punishment belt, piles of lockboxes
missing keys, jars of Nescafé, VHS tapes of Burmese pop singers

daughter #3 listens to father's records in the den
altered music room

sits on the piano bench near the door, the father in armchair
Joni singing *A Case of You*

forest *nat* flutters above in air smoky from Kent 100s

Spirit House (three)

only son trapped in
premonition, whispers

in the ear, a leap
from above

asleep on cement flower bed
rooms emptied of spoons

ankles sprained, warnings in
the head, mother offering

to the *nat* on the ground floor
honey, rice, roses

MRI Scan

band marches through the crowd

chimes gongs

a sound bridge

vibration of metal coils

there were drummers & wailing

promise of salvation

malediction but no misfortune

there were seekers & preachers

panic button

bang bang

last sensation

Bone (pantoum)

the bones of a woman the marrow groans
aches & breaks a fissure a furrow
scraping & grating bone against bone
detachment of hips dislocation of sorrow

aches & breaks a fissure a furrow
the brakes of the car an unsettling sound
detachment of hips dislocation of sorrow
align the axle your fluids are down

the brakes of the car an unsettling sound
grating & scraping of weight-bearing hips
align the axle your fluids are down
dark cherry juice in drops & drips

grating & scraping of weight-bearing hips
osteoblasts & osteocytes
dark cherry juice in drops & drips
honeycomb cartilage something's not right

osteoblasts & osteocytes
scraping & grating bone against bone
honeycomb cartilage something's not right
the bones of a woman the marrow groans

Bottle

chickens crossing, here & where
why why

laughter inside fist
of grabber

extension, arm reaching
for platters of eggs & jam

village of medicine bottles
amber & blue

she runs on four legs along a dry
river bed, mother sleeping

the sun blinking
the scar questions

why why the chickens
why why jam & eggs

why why the hand
caught in a bottle of laughter

Imaging Center

the pointer stick she grips
trails my twisting spine

she plots movement
with the exactness of a fingertip

slow as the motion of a snail in love
my naked back on treatment table

coolness hardening into memory

Hospital

tinctures for pain, capsized vessels
hand reaches into warm body
she believes in magic & so do I
painted things

riotous hips & ribcage, a being filled with liquid
stop stop now   please continue over is it
sleeping twins, lost in desert, found in hospital
pointed things

trinkets & sceptres & waterfalls in Brazil
dragon fruit scooped into bowls
owls & blue spaces in parking lots   a slithering towards
planted things

Room Tone

1. touched by an ankle
2. ballistic missile, buttercup, long lost relative
3. two felt bags, in one pearl onions, in another a book on
   Sufi masters
4. river of oil, iris box
5. the president pulled a long thin worm from the soil,
   moist & unforgiving
6. lung shade
7. *In a forest where there is no heart-wood, the castor-oil plant rules*
8. CAT scan reveals almond shape on spine
9. ferns of Kamakura, deer of Nara

A State of Mind

bruise around scar, majesty of magenta
if magenta were frosted Swiss teacakes
if majesty were sugar

scar is frosted mountain peaks
in the Alps
children's fingertips in frosting

magenta is a state of mind
where teacakes hang from firs
messengers rooted in a majesty of scars

The Soft Part of the Brain

we ride our wooden bicycles along the dust path

blooms above weep drops of sap on arms & legs

children on electric scooters zip across freeways

bring your toothbrush   memorize the cue cards

the soft part of the brain fits into a clear jar

glazed wheels   roads taken   minty pillows

Bone

the car brakes

unsettles sound

fissure & furrow

a detachment of hips

moans at home

unshakeable aches

caffeine in spleen

rods & planes

a walking stick

metal in mouth

honeycomb cartilage

over & out

the cane's from Burma

Spirit House (four)

sibling follows
sibling into
forest of thorn

girl holds stick
of incense tip aglow
37 *nats* await atop Mount Popa

volcanic relics
sister brother
blue-throated barbets

lightning clue
nest lands on soft earth
entwined vines

distant blaze
candle wick floating
in bowl of oil

Huts

the first fall
brings salty figs
brisk flowers
imaginary huts
cows hide treasures
under their tongues
& the butchers
will find gold hay
in their bellies

I have no breasts
but two dark
drops of hillside
I can never tell when it's fall
the other night
at the laundromat
the stars were huts
& I wanted to move there
become a hut & a tulip

Phone Booth

a Brownie camera slung around a sweaty neck

telephone wires crisscross

you didn't hear that did you? you did now didn't you?

child in a burlap cape leaps through the garden

three wild hogs & a mild cat

black & white self-portraits in bathroom mirrors

sun burns skin off foreheads

history has had its way

Factory

blindfold wound around a bleeding head
sepia timecards & combination locks

sound of coworkers arguing in the bathroom
or the other way around

crows captured in dim light
murder mystery for a limited audience

pupils of soft brazen green
lacquerware box in an abandoned mall

factory workers assembling cell phones & wheelchairs
a scorpion in the break room

Restaurant

I recognize her voice because it's my voice
I don't know that name because it's his name
I think your voice has a name but it's my name
she met herself in a restaurant

it wasn't her restaurant but it was a place she had been before
she had eaten eggs there, Potatoes Anna
the dishes had no names
the waiter had a high voice

how could you not remember me? we were married last May

the cakes were baked by professionals

one of them looked like a marvelous dress

what will you bring to the table? what is your sir, name?
    what are the camels doing here?

please, change, for, me

are those your wind chimes?

Diorama

where will the deer sleep? I thought about this last night
    as I always do

why do we hope? *hope & beauty are obsolete constructs*,
    they concurred

how does a painting speak? language is the difference
    among three things

who enters the spectacle? the brave ones with their silk skirts

the dining room table was set for six, one missing spoon

my neighbor captures escaped bees with a butterfly net

forest burns a violent red, deer leap from the flames, singed flanks

hold on now to what's left

Shops

phytomineral etudes
at the paw quilt shop

    nocturnal haloes
    mind fevers

smelling salts
air guitar & filigree

    why the rapidly moving notes?
    why the boxing mentors in July?

the reverie of mobs as the architects
listen for their Ganesh ringtones

Eggs

rabbits fill the boulevards
pink hue to the air
rose flush to the cheeks
chocolate eggs in abundance

plants need light to grow
rooms need light to think
cakes think best in rooms
potatoes stir underground

the cement heat rises through her sandals
she eats chocolate eggs by the handful
lacking passion
sight she takes for granted

the floor is rusty red
a woman dicing potatoes slices the earth open
at the center a tulip made of dark chocolate
she peers inside

The Parlors

a local reported to authorities that a moose
stormed downtown & broke the shop windows

ping pong was back
the bars, the halls, the parlors

shopkeepers hid their porcelain figurines
we wore bright colors to disorient the animals
wool rugs flapped open to take in the glass

the radio warned of impending drought
librarians shook their heads
elders walked through the mall in silence

half-closed eyes followed the bouncing white balls in smoky rooms
another scratchy song on the jukebox

the moose swung its mighty body through town
we continued to swing our arms & throw another one back

Spirit House (five)

as a child I did not climb trees
instead I gathered leaves that flew to the ground
the elms were tall in the fall
the neighbor boys, cruel
one left a dead kitten in a box on the doorstep

I made homes among the leaves
safety in gold, yellow, brown
invented a family who lived in a tree house
green twig, the mother
broken branch, the father

two ferns, the missing sisters

Convention Center

miniature show dogs

with bejeweled collars

& tricked up vests

sometimes their tails

get caught in the swinging hoops

causing grief & regret

I growl to my brother over the phone

how I miss the loving barks

of our childhood

Office in Lovelock, Nevada

looks like her (those tarantula-legged eyebrows)
looks away to remember

walks into carpeted office
meat-eating flowers lightning rods

the file cabinets of her brain fly open
a flush of white-out fumes

she at the keyboard in uniform
a different she holding a delivery package

both turn away to forget

Containers

what about the spitting cobra

why do I repeat myself

does self storage matter

are your teeth still here

who do you hold

is this a panic attack

when do the cormorants arrive

where does guilt come from

do you see the calathea

what disturbs me

I witness each body through the missing bricks

Relationship

when they met it was murder
was it her eyes that slayed him
lambent grenades

maybe it was the way she rolled her cigars
knowing fingers, slowly kneading
folding, pinching

love apple, love beads, love child, love feast
love grass, love-in, love knot, lovelock
love cannot be much younger than the lust for murder

she loved the way her fingers linked around his neck

Cave

moment dark
in nightclub dip

rock, heart, cave
stalagmites & echo

water drops ping
stalactites & retreat

one night I wake
sleeping body beside me

no recall of this room
this bed this person

objects signify safety
pillow, cup, watch

Portal

intersection of vine & trapeze

the white substance poured

from her mouth last night

jug tipping   spilling onto tile

eye that repeats itself in conversation

with other eye

sleep less   suspenders

another gift from Aunt Jinny

neighbor plays cello

The Swan floats through silk drapes in hallways

extreme isolation exerts a person

radio between stations

Den

in the den he would say *just keep your big mouth shut*
& we did standing in a line along the wall

I have taught you many things
at the conference I said I was God

mother would say *someday you'll meet your older sisters*
pray to Buddha, pour water in this bowl

she worked like a dog, like a dog
she loved him the most

I don't want to leave you without a father
your aunt's favorite color is blue

she'd sprinkle curry powder on our mac 'n' cheese
I'll stay with him until your sister gets married

The Cellars: A One-Act Play

SETTING
Star Zone, an abandoned nightclub in Wilmington, California.
Late 80s. Three characters stand on stage equidistant from each
other. Long strands of twinkling blue and green lights hang
from above.

CHARACTER ONE
the delirium
of blotter kippers froth
& lustrate wildly   blindly
(bedabble shale & wallow in the mist)
festal brides & clamlike fairies

    CHARACTER TWO
    ziggurats of slabber
    & air-built cellars
    unfurl the sparge & kyle
    of siccative welkins
    bedew savanna

      CHARACTER THREE
      behold:
      the froth of bedabbled fairies!
      the blotted kippers!
      the wallowing savannas!

CHARACTER ONE
a welkin in the hole
on a kyle in a kipper
slabbers the ziggurats
fane the shale willows, dear boys

CHARACTER TWO
bedabble the unfurled
& unfold
the froth of sparge
alit on a morning dew
w/ the babies
& the hugger muggers
& the landlubbers
(blotted & bedewed)
w/ sparkling pallium
delirium   bewildered

CHARACTER THREE
air-built & saucy welkins
unfurl in the froth
of littoral bugbears
the blotted cellars & roscid
crimkum crankum of fane fairies
clamlike in the cellar
(a whisper to mother or father)

CHARACTER ONE
aloft & aloof
w/ the frosty lustrates of savannas
in georgia
(our festal minds)

  CHARACTER TWO
  she hugs the mugs on the ziggurat of pickwickian cellars
  she is bedewed on a landlubber
  a littoral rillet of a circumfluous sparge
  kyle! hey kyle, sorry I didn't email you back! how ya been?

    CHARACTER THREE
    she is roscid (repeat)
    air-built (complete)
    bedabbled (indeed)

      TOGETHER
      behold the pickwickian cellars!

Spirit House (six)

the *nats* had moved into the house on Inya Lake

zoomed through halls with pocket knives,
   tamarind seeds, green bananas

family offerings of jade bracelets, cheroot cigars, deer tails

medium danced wildly in living room, drunk on palm wine
   spinning, spinning

orchestra of circle drums & copper bells played on the staircase
   nat pwe

eight children on the floorboards, leaping over uncles & cousins
   shaking, shaking

mother lit candles on the wall shrine

she spoke to the blue winged insects

     they whispered back

a *nat* warmed itself by the flame

auntie walked in a dream state

hot room

cousin slowly opened a large trunk of teak & silver strips .

the *nats* flew inside, one after the other after the other

NOTES

The Vase poems were written for a public art project for Cedar Street Gallery in conjunction with Chanda Beck's ceramics and curated by Sara Lisch. cedarstreetgallery.com

"Which gives the outer pair the heavy look of bronze clothes on statues"; "When the galley convicts clanked out of the prison in their chains"; "Desolation appears greater when pinpointed by light"

    These three poems are inspired by the film *Un Chant d'Amour*, a film by Jean Genet, 1950. Their titles are lines from the novel *Querelle* by Jean Genet, 1947.

"The eye may allow some confusion"

    The lines from this poem are from *Querelle* by Jean Genet, 1947.

"Relationship"

    The line in italics in the third stanza is from *Reflections on War and Death* (1918) by Sigmund Freud.

"Portal"

    The Swan, written by Camille Saint-Saëns in 1886, is one of 14 parts of "The Carnival of the Animals."

ACKNOWLEDGMENTS

Thanks to the editors and staff of the following journals in which some of these poems have appeared, sometimes in different versions: *The Cortland Review, Michigan Quarterly Review, Queen Mob's Teahouse, The Laurel Review, GUEST, Mekong Review, MiGoZine, Colossus: Home, Poetry International, Mary: A Journal of New Writing, speCt!, Talking Writing, 2River, Big Bridge, Glass, Be About It, F213, An Anthology,* and *They Rise Like A Wave: An Anthology of Asian American Women Poets.* Some of the poems in this book have appeared previously, also in different versions, in *Score and Bone* (Nomadic Press) and *Ruins of a glittering palace* (SPA/Commonwealth Projects).

I extend my deepest gratitude to Rusty Morrison for her gift of time, editorial expertise, and belief in my work. Heartfelt thanks to Kayla Ellenbecker, Rob Hendricks, Laura Joakimson, Ken Keegan, Trisha Peck, and the Omnidawn community.

I am indebted to Rebecca Black, Heather Bourbeau, Yvonne Campbell, MK Chavez, Steve Gilmartin, Lael Gold, Laurie Kirkpatrick, Amanda Moore, Pam Shen, Chris Stroffolino, and Tim Xonnelly for their careful reading of this manuscript and ongoing encouragement.

Enormous thanks to beloved members of my writing groups: Lea Aschkenas, Christopher Cook, George Higgins, Connie Hale, Kathleen McClung, Vince Montague, Peggy Morrison, and Anne Walker.

Further gratitude to these lovely folks for their friendship and support: Youssef Alaoui, Laura Arendal-Zacarias, Barbara Berman, Sara Biel, Jenny Bitner, Aileen Cassinetto, Sharon Coleman, Paul Corman-Roberts, Rohan DaCosta, Dayamudra Dennehy, Rae Diamond, John Dobson, Laurie Ann Doyle, Jack Foley, David Holler, Claudia Holm, Vanessa Hua, Susan Ito, Lee Romer Kaplan, Mari L'Esperance, Connie Post, Paul Quin, Bridget Quinn, Lisa Rosenberg, Martha LaMair, Kim Shuck, Margaret Stawowy, Marjorie Sturm, Kimi Sugioka, ko ko thett, Audrey T. Williams, and Megan Wilson.

Along with my collaborator, Bonnie Kwong, many thanks to the Critical Refugee Studies Program for the University of California Critical Refugee Studies Grant and to BAMPFA and the Richmond Art Center for their support of events in conjunction with this project which would not have happened without the vision and commitment of Penny Edwards.

Grateful acknowledgment to Robert Hass and Lyn Hejinian for their sponsorship as a 2019 Visiting Scholar in the Department of English at University of California, Berkeley. Special thanks to Steven Black who helped me navigate the various libraries on campus.

I am also grateful for the arts and literary communities and spaces in the Bay Area, poets and writers, organizers and curators, editors and publishers, bookstores, and art spaces for their continued commitment and hard work.

Much appreciation to my teaching colleagues of many years.

To my musical collaborators Amanda Chadhaury (Pitta of the Mind) and Evan Karp (Vata & the Vine) for their inspiration.

To Qiao Dai for her scholarship.

To Annabelle Port for her beautiful photographs.

To Kenneth Wong for his Burmese translations and advice.

To my younger sister Thet, thank you.

Forever grateful to my longtime friends, Adrian de la Peña and Mark Dutcher, for their creative camaraderie and inspiration over the years.

Love always to my partner in time, Thomas Scandura.

Finally, I am grateful to my mother, Ayya Gunasari, for whom this book is dedicated. I admire her strength and determination. Much love and appreciation for our family and extended family.

Maw Shein Win is the author of the chapbook *Score and Bone* (Nomadic Press) and the full-length collection *Invisible Gifts: Poems* (Manic D Press). She was a 2019 Visiting Scholar in the Department of English at the University of California, Berkeley and a co-recipient of the Critical Refugee Studies Grant. Win is the first poet laureate of El Cerrito, California (2016 – 2018). She teaches in the Bay Area and often collaborates with visual artists, musicians, and other writers. For more information visit www.mawsheinwin.com

Storage Unit for the Spirit House
Maw Shein Win

Cover art: *Spirit House in Transverse,* 2019, spray paint, graphite, paint marker
on canvas, 24 x 20 inches. Courtesy of the artist
Adrian de la Peña (www.adrianjdelapena.com)
Ink illustrations by Mark Dutcher, 2019

Cover and interior typefaces: Adobe Garamond, Knockout, Poetica

Cover and interior design by adam b. bohannon

Printed in the United States
by Books International, Dulles, Virginia
On 55# Glatfelter B19 Antique
Acid Free Archival Quality Recycled Paper

Publication of this book was made possible in part by gifts from
Katherine & John Gravendyk in honor of Hillary Gravendyk,
Francesca Bell, Mary Mackey, and The New Place Fund

Omnidawn Publishing
Oakland, California
Staff and Volunteers, Fall 2020

Rusty Morrison & Ken Keegan, senior editors & co-publishers
Kayla Ellenbecker, production editor & poetry editor
Gillian Olivia Blythe Hamel, senior editor & book designer
Trisha Peck, senior editor & book designer
Rob Hendricks, *Omniverse* editor, marketing editor & post-pub editor
Cassandra Smith, poetry editor & book designer
Sharon Zetter, poetry editor & book designer
Liza Flum, poetry editor
Matthew Bowie, poetry editor
Jason Bayani, poetry editor
Juliana Paslay, fiction editor
Gail Aronson, fiction editor
Izabella Santana, fiction editor & marketing assistant
Laura Joakimson, marketing assistant specializing in Instagram & Facebook
Ashley Pattison-Scott, executive assistant & *Omniverse* writer
Ariana Nevarez, marketing assistant & *Omniverse* writer
SD Sumner, copyeditor